PO3TRYJO

Growing Pains

ALEX MURDOCK

Content

CHAPTER 1: FIRST THERE WAS LOVE

A new day
Thick and thin
Halo glow

CHAPTER 2: AS IT BLOSSOMS

In thought of you
Sweet and sour
Could you be my Valentine

Oh contrary

Your eclipse

Endless ambitions

Trivial in thought

Lovers moon

 Smoke screens

Sad name grey

Life takes

Cold Summer
Journey and thoughts

Mind's eye
Wisdom rain
A mother's way
All about you
The chosen

CHAPTER 3: LOVE POISON

Scars so shallow
Dark affliction
Like a rainbow
Love swells
All sparks
In the rhythm of the night

As it stands
Stay inspired
Streaming
Life force
Resilience
What once was
What is life?
Mass that plays
Love remains
Those were the times

CHAPTER 4: DARKNESS BLOOMS

Scars that bind
Moments of torment
Love churns
I've got the blues Universal

Shepard Because of you

Divine Nature

Love Stains Elevational

Perseverance

If only

Bewilderment

In time

In the end
Lively ventures
Solitude and relief
Love lost
Affection

CHAPTER 5: DARKNESS REIGNS

Mask that wears us
Behind closed doors
If only they knew
Pain with meaning
Words
I'm not a star
I can feel your pain
Vision of mine
Memories in kindness
Sweet epicentre
Dark nightmare
Slang
Through growth
Witness the draft coming in

 Eternity
Sweetest nights

Just a vibe
In thought
In the distance

Entanglement
In the momentum

Reminiscent
In time

Timid intuition

Little did they know

Those were the days

Love remains

CHAPTER 6: PAIN REMAINS

Scars that binds

Tartarus

Cold summer
Life giveth
Those are the times

God complex

Beautiful shade

Beautiful Illusions

The hat fits

Grey traits

Tragic
Dark Continuous

Daunting tides

 Life process

Wild

Ground hog
Abysmal
Love trails
From whence we came

Black rose

Greatness
Dark origins
Time will tell
The conveying journeys

Painted Pain
Searching for you
Belly of the best
In your constellation
A sonnet to the stars

Stay in the moment

 Escapism

Chapter 7:WISDOM RAIN

Ink mode

Solar flare
Inverted
Varied time

Advantage and terrain

Instincts

Nitpicking
Back in Disarray
Control with finesse
Don't forget you
Comes and goes with the tide
Last of the Mohicans
As I decompose
Never let them get to me
Let the cold in
Where logic meets emotion
The murder of reminisce
Until I see you again
Get your free Short story Into the Abyss E-Book About Author

Get your free copy

Kane began to thrive as he attempted to make a new start with his family. He was

happy for the first time in what appeared to be a lifetime of hardship. Little did he know that the web of turmoil was still in play. Will he be able to recover from yet another daunting situation to rescue his loved ones.

Get a free copy of the sequel
Into the Abyss Volume 2
Subscribe to website for newsletter:
https://dreamimagineexpress.mailchimpsites.com/

CHAPTER 1: FIRST THERE WAS LOVE

Balance in your shade

Lemon made,

with such a sweet face.

Sweet and delicate to the taste,

a drift of drama,
with a hint of shade.

Balance in your aura,

your Psyche demands it.

I see the calming in your trance,

meticulously put together.

Powerful,

yet simple romance.

Ironically,
it was your scent of transparency,

that improved my clarity.

Now I've realised,

I am where I need to be.

Elegance

The Sun spins,

energising your wingspan.

Graceful,
in the midst of it all.

You appear to belong.

Angelic features,

so loving,
so strong.

I Need you

Destination?

The sweet beckoning,

unrelenting...

The calling to get back to you.

Far away for too long,

too long to remain strong,

inverted motivation,

causing intermittent questions,

for the lack of your mentions.

Love Conspiracies

Love conspiracies,

through your lens I find sight.

Consequently it breathes life,

in me,
then I follow.

An eager need to want to uplift you.

Tapping into the untold,
for you are mystery in love form.

Luminous in sight,

effervescence that fills to the brim.

An eventful redeem in your approximate.

Colourful and attractive,

I make myself at home,

I think I might stay.

Mind- state convoluted until the current,

but here you are,
suddenly it all makes sense.

My sire,

elemental,

your eminence.

At Peace

Life in your Grasp.

Finally Unmasked.

All i see is you.

Filling in the puzzles of my psyche.

You made it happen,

you made it whole.

No more stickiness to the surface,

gluing of pieces,
trying to make me whole again.

Find a way

Our love will find a way,

to make you stay.

I watch you lay,
eyes on drink mode everyday,

stirring,

hoping not to wither away,

like tooth decay.

Be what we envision day-by-day,

brainstorming,
feelings on pause,

revealing,

while you take my breath away.

Yet I remain

Emotions reclined to find hope.
I felt like I was losing my special place.

Without a trace,
it would up and disappear on occasions.

I would up and seek just the same.

Although fortune would never follow.

Hollow,

yet I remain.

While mind in a state of ulcers and stains,

yet I remain,

yet I remain.

The ultimate

Levitation when you speak.

Words spawn and grow wings,

like a blue bird,
love the way she sings.

Life swings from sorrow,
in your mention I breathe a better tomorrow.

The blossoming,
Shall render our love the ultimate.

For you I dare say... Special.

Watching you go, sweet memories, calling to me.

A sweet and sour situation.

Yet, smiling in spite.

 Sweet sorrows,

watching you go.

Sweet epicentre

Intoxicating in exhilarating fashion,

then here comes the passion... Like a never-ending song;
it goes on.

Melancholic vibrations began to dissipate,

let the pandemonium be our making,

muscle shakes,
efforts reverberates.
Aura ever amazing,

effervescence,
let us flow to the moon.

Maybe soon,

our bubble will burst,

and quench our thirst.

Alleviate our quakes,

whatever way it takes.

Enveloping

The calm before the storm,
Recruiting the ever burning to keep you warm,

fireplace,

laced space,

 engulfed with your beauty all over my face.

The romance.
Existing in the many trance,

a mere spark in your glance.

To be or not to be.

A step between the norm (al).

Divide and conquer,

unlike heaven what spawns.

We don't have to be perfect but we have to be honest,

in the knowing of the lines drawn,
ergo,

no malice.

Pivotal to know what bears weight for I relate,

in goodness and for the sake,
my sanity demands it,
resulting of the logic that swarms it,

epitomising.

In the pit,
waist deep,

unable to cut and release,

liquor in it's content,

begging me for a drink.

Here we go

Last night

Sweet mentions from whence you came.

Lingering DNA.
Sweet sensual decay,
time lingers,
in your mentions,
On and on...

Yours and mine

Inspiration breathes life.

Emotions cultivates,

 the need to strive.

Life long love grooms in warmth.

Daunting.

Perspective wanting.

Love flows,
from my pores to yours.

Dark connections

Walking in the mist of the night,

 darkness my only company.

all smiles,

all around me.

A sudden urge to get to know.

Clinging to my shadow.

 Whispering from ear to ear.

Feasting on our nightmares.

Party Animal

No rules.
Just loose.

Loving a pool of cools.

Unruly fool.

Working tool.

Mode on mule.

Nostalgic times

Sirens ringing,
Once upon a time whenever your name was mentioned.

Unlike the present,
where everything is so different.

The pivotal beginning of me and you,

where I was in constant awe.
In constant reminisce of you.

A roam like a comb,
a tone soaring through my chromosomes,

Heart racing,

reverberating like the skip of a beat,

raking through my very soul.

So immense,
I dispense in sense of meaning,

perhaps destiny with a smile.

A new day

Passion is our world,

the water on our plants,

sand beneath our feet.

The hope that beckons us every time we meet;

to become something more,

something special,
extra- ordinary.

A spawn of hope,
ferocious in ideals and ambition,
with an ultimate spark every time you're mentioned.

Those love stains,
memories of being shackled are no more.

Life is special,
in the absence of sorrow.

In my mind frame I remain,
in the eye of my subconscious there is optimism,

constant.

Thick and thin

Who would have thought it was meant to be,

yet here we are.

Solace,
gripping at your conscious,

so sensitive to my intentions,
but safe in the expectations of what may come,

 for I am no stranger to putting you at ease.

You have grown savvy as a result of being privy to all possibilities;

for when it comes to you and me,
like similes,
bouncing from one to another,
like it was ordained.

Reciprocation in kind,
for a great mind is hard to find,

special in light of my company,

even the stars would breathe in envy.

Halo Glow

Sweet memories are like a halo over thee.

Feeling abashed,
a result of mental spillage on your approach.

intertwined by the rays that shine.

Special are the days we find hard to pack away;
in our trunks with trinkets of the beautiful innuendos smothered by your
DNA.

So the memories dawn.

The shine,

unrefined,

commence to filter into mine.

CHAPTER 2: AS IT BLOSSOMS

In thought of you

Hope to make you smile.

On a cloud shouting out loud.

Hoping my word will bounce around,

in and out of town;
back to you,
my hope and intention,

objective for an incentive.

An infectious energy,

a residue of my smile.

My aura calling for you,

hoping you will respond...

Causing clinical effervescence,

that slips between your mentions.

Memorial recall;
in your sad times,

 sudden and instant regurgitation,

then a smile for a while.

Sweet and soar

Lemonade shade.

Darkness fades.

Nature spells,

enveloping smells.

Enticing,

hoping for me to stay.

Summer trails,
exuberant tales Compelling...
Although only temporarily can I remain,

your painful chains,
prove too much for us to maintain.

Could you be my Valentine

Beauty is in the eye of the beholder,

and so I told her...
Come closer,
so I can see the special in you.

She remain timid,
yet engaged by my pursuit..

Still calm,

 driven by the storm... In you

So sweet,

happy,

 glad to meet.

Experience brings treasures,

memory defining treats.

Finally,
she approaches,

 wanting to know.

Despite her dismay.

Giving her a smile,

 realising a future,

 our vision,

on valentines day...

Oh Contrary

If(s) and maybe(s),
can flow so "oh contrary"...

A hail Mary

To be or not to be,

continually.
Life's innuendos and charm.

Irrevocably,
it appears and seems to be.

It is,

 irrespective of want.

Leg stretchers,
beautiful path,
the eventual defining of adventures.

Such as the wanting(s) that keeps me easing into leisure...

So we ponder,

 wait,

accompanied by life,

and yours sincerely.

Heart,

beat in deceit,

"Oh contrary".

Your Eclipse

Mood,
dimmed by the fading sunlight,

quietly taking flight.

A flip and a fright,
a sense of foreboding as darkness shivers,

 eclipsing the escaping yet fading...

Entertaining nevertheless,

 unimpressed but it brings a welcoming zest.

Making stress less,
as I continue in my waiting.

Unbeknownst to what or whom,
until the moment,
the thought of seeing you soon.
Life has never been the same without your lame,

to tame,
an unfiltered dame;
a struggle to manoeuvre around my maim,

history beckons me,

scars exposing my stories...

Should you feel the need to see.

Endless ambitions

If It pleases you,
it is incentivised and idealised,

multiplied into a thousand fold.

Unmould,
deciphered,
pieces uplifted,
customised and added to your very soul.

Your decorations,
a token of my appreciation from whence we came,

for showing me special things from a special place.

Remaining,
in moments close to the tethering of our unravelling,

teasing in the mist of our unfiltered destiny.

Getting the best of us,
words we never thought would come.

Fortunately,
the endeavour that continues to illustrate for me and thee,

a reflection of our infinite destiny.

Trivial in thought

Pondering,

psychological in wonderment.

only the special types of frequencies can catch these transverse waves.

Energy grades,
high in life with the utmost type of levels left behind,

intact and paved.

Life is consistent when you pay attention,

it purrs as it revolves,
remains in my constant.

To remain dormant in the background,

yet dominant in a passive way.

Rearing its meticulous head if only to show a wisdom tooth or two.

Surely not to recognise me?

I would impose thoughts to myself,
drowning in the allure of the immense possibilities of what this means,

or what it could be.

Lovers Moon

Lovers Moon,
howling in the intimacy of the night.

No fight nor flight.

Just our essence bearing the dark of our nightmare,

with only you to keep me fair.

Being present,

fearing my altering, to not fall and disappear,

away from you.

Mortality beckons me,

only for you to see me through.

Quenching my hopes to live eternally,

 through you.

Strengthening my reappearing,

yet tangible presence.

Smoke Screens

Uncanny semblances,

brought back memories,

only to disappoint.

For the mirror- cracks reappears at an instant.

Loneliness drew close from a distance,

unrelenting as the blood spills,

contacting inward,

and then some.

A sad name grey

Dreams.

Beams like terrestrial,
Leave 'absence' with ponder in its stead.

The want becomes apparent,

 a sudden whiff of your scent,

with a hint of the elements,

special things comes to mind,

then special would fluctuate.

A sudden thought nevermind,

realising it's simply ponder and wonderment.

Withdrawn.
Fighting the urge of a sudden spawn,

robust with merit,

unwilling to inherit,

feelings of dismay,

a sudden lay,

creeping like decay,

a peppermint hint,
causing a sprint and a spray from mental,

leaving me shouting to let the pain spray.

Deluded in the desire to let it go,

and so...

This day looking so grey and hollow,

I feel the need to let you know...

Special is the name of my sorrows.

Life takes

Walking on a different plain,

unbeknownst the need to retreat to the subconscious.

The feeling,
the need to re-acclimate,
life has been unwilling to be the same...

Still I smile, speak not so callous.

Winds remains ever so warm,

if only for what it desires.

However,
Rippling as the constraints drown in unsavoury surroundings,

the unfazed proving to be rebelling,
seizing to believe in.

Perhaps I am not worthy for their season,

 their sparking eyes to continue to pave the way.

If only to continue,
to allow and not be lead astray.

Unlike the here and now,

situated within the dark.

Not a blink,

barely a spark.

Thus,

struggles.

Nevertheless,
thought breathless,
I smile in the struggle to make my mark.

Cold summer

Elementary,
in a sense of simplicity,

conveying how much you mean to me.

Head quiz,
a juxtapose at times,

 lacking consistency,

unlike how much you feel for me;

in a sense it stays,
it sits and ponder,

a wonderland,
a special place you've made...

Beautiful with extra summer,

and extra shade.

Unlike the past,
we are what we want to be,

and to know of.

What is?
You can clearly see.

Ordinance with clarity.
The future is not an unnatural contemplation,

it is encouraged to breathe,

exhaling with ease,

slow releases,

careful to check for a pulse,

then with a skip of a beat,

off she goes.

A beautiful trend,
with so much to say,

relaying your every thought,

Checking the temperature;
it ranges between extremes like the weather,

and so I never leave without my specifics;

though ever the critic,

I dare not attempt to predict the unpredictable,

for your under-layers remain well hidden.

What is life?

The subconscious.

 It holds everything;

your every persona,

everything you are.

And so we hope that life takes over,

make your memories an adventure,

embarking of various endeavours.

Love,
heart breaks,
the not so forgetful pusses,

the tall tales with roots that quakes,

in your presence,
for the relevance still bleeds.

Like seeds,
it is rooted within me.

I am sired to my destiny and it is on to me.

Such are the conquest of intellectual spontaneity,

a calling for discovery.

I want to be more,

my mind says to me,

begging the question.

Will time remember thee?
Thy calling,
to be something other than perceptive normalcy.

A superman known for a super- mind,

a lack of brawn on my name,

intellectuality,

all over me.

So I query what is meant for me? Carrying on,
till deaths do us part,

death doors walked into being reborn.

Journey and thought

Ready for the journey,
for I admire all that life entails.

Despite the odd winter trails,

surprised by their occasional showing.

Leaving me at its mercy,

nobody to save me,

not even myself.

Special are the times that slips into our hearts,

alleviate sleepless nights,

unravelling the prideful tides.

To put a smile,
a sunny mantle piece on the midst of displease,

in the moments that we seek not be mentioned,

but holds relevance,

and so you know.

For you,
special continue to show,

embraced from different dimensions,

then dare to care.

Mind's Eye

Wailing at the impaling,

implant from your progressive,

regressive and ultimate demise.

Unfortunate nonetheless,

every blessing thought of your rest.

 forever in mind,

and deservingly so,

 halt to a crawl,

mind grows weary while losing control.

What was meant to be is no more,
the thought of forever just a figment of thought.

Wisdom rain

After all,
going through it have me delirious,

 less serious;

thick- skinned to the cause.

Continuity for a while then the odd pause,

 recalling,
trying to unpack from small-in.

The need for understanding to have a conversation,

in my mention,
direct or indirectly,

any will suffice,
allowing my cognitives to take over,

let wisdom rain,
withering away my tearful memories.

Similarly,
having faith,
knowing that the universe will come for me,

disperse into bite-size,
to show a tell of what is necessary,

something that is a need to see...

So finally, understanding brings fourth,

eagerness grows in the need to know,

revelations brings fourth healing in the presence of clarity.

A mother's way

Earthly,
unlike the seasons love transcends.

 Thought never scorned.

Grooms in the brightest lights or dullest of dawn.

Love drawn from a nipple,

or swallowed from a spoon.

Adapting,

mending in the midst of pain,

finding the courage to pull through.

The will to carry on,
inspired from whence you were born.

Motherly,
dazed and wonder in amazement,

at the will to prevail.

All about you

In thought about you,

everything to pursue,

it flows to mind.

Elevational in a motivating fashion,

new discoveries in light of passion...

Unrelenting peaks,
never seeking but inevitably revealing...

"You're special" I would blindly speak within,

then reiterate in contemplation of everything you do...

Everything you are.

Unsullied by the purity of your convictions,

I could remain in my stance,

continuing to go on,
and so in my pursuit to reveal all to you...

Invigorating,
in thought of your growth and mine,

spirits will remain in kind.
All about you.

The chosen

Life's long dream,

so pivotal it seems,

reign to remain supreme.

Not faltered by the strain to make one's desires come true,

 but secretly scripting lessons to one day draw wisdom.

 To lay at the door of dismay and to make one pay;

the ultimate homage to what the universe and what nature has put into
play,
for we are the resulting relish of the one thing all seeing and unbeknown to
any,
yet the impact containing unrestrained by the strength of what it packs with
the ultimate revealing.

Heavenly is the word amongst the thieves.
As the holy relish in the devil like antics of the not knowing in blissful
ignorance.
Life.

CHAPTER 3: LOVE POISON

Scars so shallow

Love was made for me and you,

unrelenting.

Mutually sensing,
sensual scent in,
feasting in the eyes and hearing...

The feeling,

approximate revealing...

Spontaneity in your shielding,

ducking and diving,

be hold,
the emotion,

alien to the thick-skinned of your sensation,

thus the following...

The retrieval of memories that follows,

behold the narrows,
that climb off the walls that were built in,

and so hollow.

Tread with care fallen on deaf ears,

 and so apparent the rest of the years...

Sequential regrets and nightmares.

Dark affliction

To discover,

 to uncover,

 to unravel.

If there is such a thing.

Brain storming.

What is...
The scars that swallows,

 bleeds me hollow,

oozing with fear.

Life applauds my open consciousness,

in light of my nightmare.
In open atmosphere,

breathing,

 unfair,

 life tales.

Leaning backwards,
hoping for a retreat within my own shadow.

Like a rainbow

Like a rainbow in the sunlight,

 staying afloat because of you.

In your absolute there lives truth,

thereby keeping me real.

Blooming in your sunlight,

Sane in the current,

it moves in such relentless,

senses perplexed,
but faithful in the feeling emanating.

Love swells

Love swells in your presence,

metastasizing.

Divide and multiply.

Epidemic like,

flattering symptoms.

On sort of special acts follows,

 because of you.

All sparks

Colour play,

fireworks.
All sparks in your presence.

Unwilling to forget your name,
in the fear life would never be the same.

Sweet sense,

snaps,

complexes are all i know with you...

The world sparks because of you.

In the rhythm of the night

In the rhythm of the night.

 Searching for the one thing,

 something.

To allow the surrender of my plight.

Scrutiny,

it dawns on me,
yet actions comes naturally.

Organically,
it all applies to me.

Special things that you are,

glowing as it flows.

Our cosmic flames will never die,

in the rhythm of the night.

As it stands

The air stands still.
I close my eyes and ponder when I should wake.

Time is a fortunate page,
decade is but a quick nap in my world.

In the blink of an eye a week would go by,

eternal I stand alone.

Branching,
reaching for knowledge;
the only essence that invigorates my aspirations.

Stay Inspired

The air we breathe,

the plants we eat,

the water we drink;

that flows and waters our clothes,

from so far only universe really knows.

Inspiration and the personification of such,

it remains like stains,
all around us.
So docile and futile are seasonal activities...

Proactivity remains around us.
Times are dark,

but inspiration remains limitless.

Streaming

On route to your soul,

swimming through your stream,

hoping you remain whole.

For what I do will not be in vain,

please stay constant.

From whence I came,
it will be for the beckoning of your subconscious.

The calling to be in your mentions,

your attention blooms my soul.

Settling my cognitives,

leaving me feeling whole,
feeding on the presence of your forgiving soul.

Life force

Life force remain porous,

and so you drink away.

A welcoming stay,

here,
please have it,
a pleasant gesture to pave the way.

For sorrows are for tomorrow,

a cold winter slay.

Skating on pain,
on the road to insanity.
Picking rubber bleeding flesh all the way to the never-ending pleasures,

that resides in me.

Resilience

An accomplice to my safe haven,

 to see me through.
Keep me going and keep me true.

Coveting moments,
cutting out connotations,
pertaining to memories that once was dead to me,

 now recycled;

giving me energy.

What once was

In the process of our best moments,

I grieve in the thoughts.

Those moments that defines us are no more,

 potential absconded and moved on,
some for the best,
but I say simply due to the presence of love-less.

What is life?

Am I right or wrong,
complicating derivative of the compass between love and hate;

so much love,

one cannot help but hate,
but love demands its own space of growth and protection.

Maybe the seek for objectivity is the god within me,

to look beyond the decorations of what is,

 to what lies as the naked truth.

Perhaps the search for God is leading me to self discovery and grace
inside.
Classifications vary based on the evidence and thoughts compiled in

regards to objective interpretation.
The potential for greatness showing implication of underlying energy,

cells compelled to explode in true detonative form,

the laws of wrong and right is of no relevance.

Thus whether it is good or bad,
the only matter is the question of destiny and whom deemed it so.

Mass that plays

Little did they know,
it is laid bare,
in the dawn of the callous breeze,

intuitive in its gaze,

a sight with a focused stare.

It could have travelled for days,

within that split second.

Indecisive remnants plagues,
waiting for the day of unrelenting confidence.

Lit like a seasonal tree,

holding the weight of the universe.

I remain immersed,

pondering the inner contents of life.

The day of realisation,
we are more than we ever dreamt,
only then the whole world is allowed to see.

Love Remains

In the end it all remains;

the lame,

strain,

the passion spilt like blood stains.

A subconscious archive,

mapping the history of your pain.

There lies a stimulus,

unfiltered and robust,

what may have been your greatest love.

Now neglected and unattended,

surrounded by cobwebs,

relic of an elderly time,

from which it remains;

the telling,

entailing words of compelling.

Now read from a distance,

a composite of misfortunes and smiles,

giving relevance to once was.

Those were the times

Calm is a stranger that befits the norm.

Humbling are the thoughts of those times when my mind is inclined;

to bring cheer to my most current of times.

To sit back and relapse on when things begets a smile.

Sharing is but a reverence to another period,

I leave for you to surmise.

In the here and now time remains unkind...

Dragging and draining needs no explaining.

CHAPTER 4: DARKNESS BLOOMS

Scars that bind

Scars that bind are never hard to find.

Pusses and ulcers thrive on rapid decline.

Such as the memories that covets,

 the withering mares of the night.

Unloving shakes and earthquakes,

those were the days,

never to be relived.

Still callous to the touch,

numbing provokes unbecoming,

unfortunate that the stains remain.

Moments of torment

Our souls will never seize to wonder in the afterlife,

and so we will grow tormented,
We shall pass again in the depth of Tartarus,

where our spirits remain disconnected,
and no longer whole.

Surrounded by the undead weighted by their own ills,
unable to move on from the unfortunates moments that once was our lives,

pondering the moments of our demise.

Love churns

Romantic ties,

entangled in the complexities,

composites of various emotions.

Inhale and exhale,
just to mentally dismount and come up for air.

Perhaps one day,
I may be one,
with my emotional nightmare.

I've got the blues

A possession,
straining as it tunnels through every vein,

 on the way in.

Deeper,
soul tremor,

 leaving you pale.

Ever waned by the pain that inspires no direction.

Thus enhancing the strain,

spreading across every membrane.

Symptoms of the blues,
leaving nothing but emotional clues that never ends.

Universal shepherd

When karma calls my name,
it reiterates.
Things will never be the same,
change is but a time,
it knows your name,
It covets thee in everyday;
just as I have cherished thee when laid bare and true.
Like a mannequin for all things that holds meaning,
and through me it remains transparent with thoughts and feelings.

A reflection of all that is and yet contemplating.

For the stars are ours,
it shivers at the power we wield,
As it holds awaiting what we one day may deem;
if we ever realise our immortality and become more...

For our wings grow restless,

our true form sit still and grow sore.

Because of you

The colouristic views,

 in you. The clues ensures,

constantly you remain my muse,

even in your absence.

Residual eminence of your aura,

always present to see me through.

Without you,

could I do.

Loving,
the coming,
all because of you.

Divine Nature

The gods prithee thee;

 something extraordinary.

Thus,
my aura illuminates...

In line with nature...

Though I remain no stranger,
to the confines and infatuation that calls to my emotions.

In fact I am more convoluted by clarity,

 it finds me and pour fully,

intuition that I'd rather not be privy.

Though such are the curses that leaves you wanting,

 in search of empathy.

Love stains

Appreciatively, unequivocally.

Intimately,
in thought of intimacy;

followed by mentions of thee.

Constructive envy,

brainstorm spree,

ultimately,
wherever you are I feel the need to be.

Elevation

Seismic shifts in your mental,

your mood succumb to optimistic gains.

The weight of the world suddenly is not so daunting.

Less of the draping of blood on your shoulders,
on account of the stones and martyr in your nightmares.

The sun and the moon are once again moments,

no longer simultaneous in perception.

In your mentions life is once more.

Perseverance

Ego in a slumber,
after reminiscing on mileage of piling numbers.

Nostalgia.
Special were things of the past,

driving fast,

 and so struggling to grasp.

 Convenient as pain is known to be no saint.
Driving,

losing track of time and hours.

The urge to purge and re-submerge.

 Motivation,

and then some.

If only

When it rains it pours,

 extreme experience,

 ultimate remorse.

In the confines of life,

through times that are rife,

we strive,
to survive,
hoping the pain halts.

To not remain,
the blood stains unravel,

dark plights with might.

Increase smiles,
then further enticed to take flight.

If only.

Bewilderment

There is witchery in your being. It calls to me.

Bewildered and captivated,
and so I approximate your affections.

Little did I know they were more than just a potion;

a composites of passion and emotions,
pain and bloodstains,

residuals of unfortunate experience.

Such are the factors that dawns at your door,

awaiting my presence in contribution to my own downfall.

So am scarred,
thus my curse means I am destined to love from afar.

In time

When time has passed.
We shall see when the dark no longer knows our name.

We shall spark when the light no longer lay claim to our abilities,

 but allow them to elevate beyond the skies,
reaching new limits and new discoveries.

Laying signs to new dimensions,
for when we're the ancestors we may be remembered.

In the end

After me and you,

 will the light remain...

Will it lay across the bowels of the world and smile,

 extinguished by departure of our souls,
for in our pairing,

there lies a force that is solely treasured,

it breathes life into the universe,
to further develop and continue to immerse.

In the never ending cycle of nature and the cosmic thoughts and
implements that envelopes.

Loves of sorts,

uncanny and so remote.

Life brought to a standstill,

 to hear the unfiltered,

 and organic spill.

Lively Ventures

Life in the darkness,
and so the lessons are taught,

envelopes to be smart.

Illusions leave you in so much tremor,

you can't help but grip your heart.

Life but only knows to lay a path,

and so the journey continues,

thus we walk.

Rhythm tilted in preparation,
for so much could be on the arisen,
yet consistent for the cognitive teaches us nothing is coming.

Solitude and relief

Where do the sane go to find cane for their brain?

To soar above the sour,
the bad flavour,

for like a stain it remains.

The haunting,

ever daunting,
the path is ever unclear...

Revelling in what is portrayed,

 sensing your weaknesses,

 knowing where they remain,

pulsating,

as your fears moan in the unpredictability of what is precedes as its last living days.

The withering.
Begging for life's currencies to pay for another day.

Love Lost

The earth still sore and scorched in your departing.

Bearing memories from which your tears were drained.

Low emotions,

almost left you tamed..
Porous earth,
lamed by the melancholic ties that was yours,

though you left while it remained.

Tired and tender times wither in the ties you left behind.

Affection

Amusing as you tried,

 benign was your effort,

though it left in an effort to smile,

 at a later date.

Convoluted in sight,
still hoping for the clarity to eventually see me through.

Brewing,
nectar stewing as I create discrepancies in my descriptions to avoid my
affections for thee,
thought I find it apparent and lacking a smokescreen,
if only you knew me.

At times,
the life would implore me to convene in thought,

 is not life beautiful;
a sight I find bountiful,

in thought of you.

Escapism

I look to thee when emotions overwhelms;

petrifying climate,
the water grows ever so sore since my escape.

The Sun heated over the insanity that prevails,
but what could change unless the universe intervenes.

Paranoia runs deep,
so no time for dwelling,

only option is to stay lean.

In the forefront there you are,

navigating my escape,
if only that was so...

For at this time I lay in bloody memories,

dripped and draped.

Yesterday was but a wishful thought,

a pendulum to my unnatural state.

Now I sit and stare at my emotions,

waiting for the perfect escape.

CHAPTER 5: DARKNESS REIGNS

Mask that wears us

Calm is the norm that remains the spawn that nobody appears to grasp,

unless with the aid of,
resulting in them looking outwards from a mask.

Thus I ask,
how true are you when your true nature is hidden away?

In other words lacks transparency or failure to unravel.

Those are the trilogies we repeatedly play,

especially in times of dismay,
in the daunting plays of pain at dawn;

our hearts flicker and flip,

in the mere thought and experience that leaves us thick-skinned and dense.

Is there such a thing as heart cries,

with possibly more than one prying ear?

Perhaps.

Though the perplexed aching of your screams makes it hard to intervene,

deflecting the screening to the epicentre of your pain and fragmented lame;

melancholic juices now flowing,

and the river was born..

Yet wherever the source remains nobody will ever know,

for your are now buried deep.

Behind close doors

Having the time of your life since growing your wings.

Yet heavy is the heart that is laid bare in chained remains.

The only question to thee;

Are you really free?

For life is more,

times swings and sways with ferocity that even the seasons becomes
fatigued and sore.

Sitting in thought,

contemplating...

Is it possible to live a life behind closed doors?

If only they knew

When it happens you will know,

when effective it will show.

Life long lines;
aged unsettling and reflectively refined,
telling your stories on your branded billboard,
which remains your authentic yet superficial that nobody can read but you.

Until one day the cracks and smokescreens starts to reap their own sewing,

leaving you exposed;
so as a result all I witness is your carnage.

To look,
to gaze,

 having you weeping, even gasping for days.

In halt trying to catch your breath,

but what is to be is to be,
and then what's not isn't.

Karma begins with questions,

 words comes to life and begin to mention,

the passion that lingers,
draped in insane,
just one opportune moment to have you in pain.

Loneliness numbs,
it runs so deep it becomes embedded,

 prone to sharpen your instincts,

especially into the unknown.

Those are the words we practice in vain.
Though one day they became the unfiltered,

 refreshing ponder of your psyche,
clutching at your heels to hear your even further unfiltered spills.

Pain with meaning

The poison in your veins makes it hard to lay,

twisting and turning,
the never-ending dismay.

Though I stare in your eyes.

Amazing!

Like an all spark,
aiding ships to ports,
in an eclipse;
watching the illumination from the days in.

All of a sudden I forget my sorrows,

focused on enduring another tomorrow.

Words

Senses.
In a feeling,
boding towards stupendous.

While polishing and cleaning my innuendos.

Sharpening my trade before putting on lay-away,

a wordsmith by day.
Wording with a tickle,
and a ground with a folly..

Susceptibility for you to fall and take your breath away.

I'm Not A Star

To be a star is to finally be who you are;
for the world precedes to feed,
from your light for so many twilight it is somewhat unprecedented.

Elemental,
I'm not a star for when I look upon you,

I see the true definition and the ultimate revealing.

Screaming!
How true you are and your being.

It has proven me worthy,
for to see the god in you,

has lead me to being,

seeing the light in me.

Revealing the skies in need for a light like me,

decreed to be yet unknown,
and so a star is born.

Thus, I shine.

I can feel your pain

I can hear the screams,
it compels my hearing;

reverberating through dimensions,

it heightens my senses.

My troubled aura constantly eyeing through the curtains.

Paranoia personified,
the very definition of expectations.

Piles of arrhythmia,
my vibrations have never been the same;
it peaks and tweaks to heights that can't be tamed.

So I sit and wait,

suffocating the need to contemplate.

I hope not too late,
as always my efforts I dare not approximate.

Doing for you is doing for my soul;

thankful the reshaping have left me unscathed.

Vision of mine

Soul of solitude.

Bordering on opportunist tendencies.

Sweet sores tingles my internal derma.

Though inoculated by a sense of calm,

in such heights,
cerebral echelon.

To peep in pond on the further beyond.

Maybe you'll remember me;
as I visit frequently.

In the hope to see,

beautiful minds,

a mere vision,

or the future of the mere eventual that one day will be a possession of mine.

At least in memory.

Memories in Kind

Your affections remains unblemished,

like your touch;
forever possessed in memory.

Still it stays,

absent of smoke or dust.

Solidified,

 eternal.

Like liquid,

 adapting,

yet viscous.

Our movements aligned,
I sense a time it may be better off.

All but a moment in need,

and growth breathes in folds,

 joined by new minds,

or memories in kind.

Reiterating the memories,

the sweet times,

since I made you mine.

Sweet epicentre

Intoxicating in an exhilarating fashion,

then here comes the passion.

Like a never-ending song; it goes on.

Melancholic vibrations began to dissipate,

 let the pandemonium be our making,

muscle shakes,
efforts reverberates.
Aura ever amazing,

effervescence,
let us flow to the moon.

Maybe soon,
our bubble will burst,

and quench our thirst.

Alleviate our quakes,

in whatever way it takes.

Dark night

The darkness came along in the midst of my unwavering transition,

faltering,
tip toeing around light in my subconscious.

Finally reached its final destination,

the point of no return.

Nobody else could see or sense the dark but me,

further relapse follows as the feeling of helplessness crept.

Sensing my disposition.

It started to smile,
then danced the whole night.

Slang

You're just a slang away from resonating;

 your mind to mine.

Thus,
I speak with purpose.

Amassing years of love and stimulus.

It continues to speak to us.

Special elements,

 now synchronised..

Leading our captivation.

Special are the times,
inclined that we stood in our company.

An out of body experience,

watching our interaction.

Like a soul floating away from us,

with a bird's eye view;

loving our meticulous clues,

weeping our chaotic times,

followed by our sweetest blues.

It speaks to us.

Through growth

Is there a place for me and you,

solely for our innermost solitude,

the remnants of our fibres finest.

 To go be alone,
to manifest in its finest glory.

So one day we can grow,
to appreciate parts of us we could only feel through growth.

Witness the draft coming in

In the midst of the echo,

there you were again.
Life treasures that I now know,

unlike the beginning.

It appeases me to ponder the various predictions;

such as the knowledge of you not being alone,

ever again.
Unless it is ordained,
which in this case would be the death of me.

Pause,
suspense,
expectant discomfort while the shivers commence.

Eternity

Enamoured by the stars,
in a pause as they succumb to an awe.

Take my breath away,

if you elect to stay if only everyday.
In the mist of my mind's eye as I reminisce,

 on what a world it would be;

if only you could see.

Life's decree,
come on a journey with me.
Lets act and re-enact all that we are and could be.

Lets be more than a theory, and ever,
and ever.

Sweetest nights

The sky comes alive at night to witness your sight.

Like a carpet refined by the night breeze,
it dips and swoops down from over the mountain.

It carries your every memory and every emotion.

Tethered by your smiles as it bears your sadness.

How sweet are the skies when you're beneath it.

Though the tremors comes at your dismay.

Hating your cries,
thought the sparks of your tears causing the wind to blow away.

Sweet soul makes darkness forgetful,
and nightmares bring less tears.

Just a vibe

If not for the strength,
I could not subscribe to something bigger than myself.

Speaking silence so my mind can talk loud.

Elevation,
beyond mere elementary fashion.

Vibe complex elevates my spirit,

 compounded by composites of hereditary tragedy.

Though it elevates my medicinal resolution in hard times.

Thus,
alleviation now that my vibe grew wings;

finally I can take flight through a hawk's eye.

In thought

Pseudo innuendos,
multiplied by fragmented passion.
Leading to the subduing of love flow,
and so it goes no more.
Life conduits of messages that weather the test of time,

like a seed it shares in kind.
Finally.
Clarity.
At a stand still.

Unkind endings

Indecent time of the unrefined,
inclined to pivot your plight for the sake of your mind.

For who are the keepers of peace,

praying when the light cease,

 we remain in the bosom of the kind.

In the distance

Anything to make the pain stay,
for the in the midst of it,
everything you are and more remain in process of rapid decay.

Memories gentrified.
Thoughts collide.
The only solvent was your final steps,
further and further away.

Entanglement

Such tangled webs we weave,
if only to approximate,
like a thousand generations of blue melancholic trees.

In the moment

Let the juices flow,
over the leaves and trees until there is no more.

Perhaps they could make sense of what is or was.

Where does time abstain,
to a happy place from this universe, from the laying claim to blame.

A day off,
a place refrained,
from the spectrum or various protrusion of life.

Take me there.

For the insistence to desist,
the many pondering that exist are too strong.

Like a band aid,
I'm engulfed by my melancholic shade.

Flashbacks through contacts,

 ill facts,
ill will make it hard to relax.

Standing in consternation.
Elevation is but a wish that never comes to pass.

Reminiscent

Mood,
all of sudden dimmed by the fading sunlight,

quietly taking flight.

A flip and a fright,

a sense of foreboding as darkness shivers eclipsing the escaping yet fading.

Entertaining nevertheless,

 unimpressed but it brings a welcoming zest.

Making stress less,
as I continue in my waiting.

Unbeknownst to what or whom,
until the moment,

 the thought of seeing you soon.

Life has never been the same without your lame,

 to tame,
an unfiltered dame;

a struggle to manoeuvre around my maim,

history beckons me,
scars exposing my stories,

should you feel the need to see.

In time

Moments have the potential of echoing forever throughout time.

Reverberating through black holes,
solar systems and even multiple universes if possible.

Those are the times,
the potential to be great.
So speak.

Timid Intuition

The road is ever- mending,
a trip and skip in time as the pain falters;
a mere play on delay on its way to another cause and effect...

And so into my conscious,

it stirs,
showing epic form,

 some what of a perfect storm.

Loving the appeal,
sometimes I ask what does that make me,

maybe am in need of an intervention,

gazing away in wonderment.

Unwilling to be wise,

waiting for the tremor,

a flicker and a spill.

Perhaps love will heal.

Time will tell.

Like a close friend,

it always reveals.

Little did they know

Little did they know,

Intuitive in the way it shows.

Hiding in decisiveness,
waiting for the day of unrelenting confidence.

We are what we are meant to be,

 lit like a seasonal tree,

holding the weight of the universe.

I remain immersed,
pondering the inner contents of life,

waiting for the day we are more than we ever dreamt was ever possible to be,
only then the whole world is allowed to see.

Those were the days

Calm is a stranger that befits the norm.

Humbling are the thoughts of those times when my mind is inclined;

 to bring cheer to my most current of times.

To sit back and relapse on when things begets a smile.

Sharing is but a reverence to another period,

 I leave for you to surmise.

In the here and now time remains unkind...

Dragging and draining,
it needs no explaining.

Love remains

In the end it all remains;
the lame,
strain,
the passion spilt like blood stains.

A subconscious archive,

mapping the history of your pain.

There lies a stimulus,

unfiltered and robust,
what may have been your greatest love.

Now neglected and unattended,

  surrounded by cobwebs,

relic of an elderly time,

from which it remains;

the telling,
entailing words of compelling.

Now read from a distance,
a composite of misfortunes and smiles,

  giving relevance to once was.

Scars that bind

Scars that bind are never hard to find.

Pusses and ulcers thrive on rapid decline.

Such as the memories that covets,

  unfazed by mares of the night.

Unloving shakes and earthquakes,

  those were the days,
never to be relived.

Still callous to the touch,

  numbing provokes unbecoming,

  unfortunate that the stains remain.

Tartarus

Our souls will never seize to wonder in the afterlife,

and so we will grow tormented.
We shall pass again in the depth of Tartarus,

where our spirits remain disconnected,

and no longer whole.

Surrounded by the undead weighted by their own ills,
unable to move on from the unfortunate moments that once was our lives,

pondering the moments of our demise.

Cold Summer

Elementary,
in a sense of simplicity,

conveying how much you mean to me.

Head quiz,
a juxtapose at times,

lacking consistency,
unlike how much you feel for thee;

in a sense it stays,

it sit and ponder,
a wonderland,
a special place you've made.

Beautiful with extra summer,

 and extra shade.

Unlike the past,
we are what we want to be,
and to know of what is you can clearly see..

Ordinance with clarity.

The future is not an unnatural contemplation,

it is encouraged to breathe,

exhaling with ease.
Slow releases,
careful to check for a pulse,
then with the skip of a beat,
off she goes...

A beautiful trend,
with so much to say,

relaying your every thought,

 checking the temperature.

It ranges between extremes like the weather,

and so I never leave without my specifics;

for I dare not attempt to predict the unpredictable,

for your under layers remain well hidden.

Life giveth

The subconscious. It holds everything;

your every persona,

everything you are.

And so we hope,
that life takes over,
make your memories an adventure,

an embark of various endeavours,

enhanced by destiny.

Love,
heart breaks,
the not so forgetful pusses,
the tall tales with a root that quakes, in your presence,

for the relevance still bleeds.

Like seeds,
it is rooted in my DNA,
I am sired to my destiny and it is on to me.

Such are the conquest of intellectual spontaneity,

a calling for discovery.

I want to be more,

my mind says to me,

begging the question.

Will time remember thee?
Thy calling,
to be something other than perceptive normalcy.

A superman known for a super- mind,

 a lack of brawn on my name,

 intellectuality,
all over me.

So I query what is meant for me?

carrying on,
till death do us part,
and death doors walked into being reborn.

These are the times

The season is pending,

wilting for the following.

Unwilling to leave things torn and turn,

for many things may falter,
and prolong.

Like a beautiful song,

it resonates,

 intermediate,

it enters my space.

Times remains unfiltered,

 thus unpredictable,

lifetime shivers...

Expectancies remain at a constant,

awaiting destiny's hand to allow a spec of dream,

in relation to life and whatever is coming,

and preordained,
eventual to occur or remain;

if only for a season.

Seasonal dismay,

utterly infectious.

Hurting,
eventual to stuck into my lonesome soul.

Brain convoluted;

 touching time,

infection in my mention.

The universe my only console,

for the moment.

God complex

Am I right or wrong,
complicating derivative of the compass between love and hate;

 so much love,
one cannot help but hate,
but love demands its own space of growth and protection.

Maybe the seek for objectivity is the god within me,

to look beyond the decorations of what is,
to what lies as the naked truth.

Perhaps the search for God is leading me to self discovery and grace within.

Classifications vary based on the evidence and thoughts compiled based on objective interpretation.

The potential for greatness showing implication of underlying energy,

cells compelled to explode in true detonative form,
the laws of wrong and right is of no relevance.

Thus whether it is good or bad,
the only matter is the question of destiny and whom deemed it so.

A God complex.

Beautiful shade

Lonely are the days I sit in a faze,

sipping on my darkness,

while self pity gave me shade.

Though no matter,
life is for living,
even in the mist of distasteful ways.

Pretty times in the confines of my mind,

as it pulls and prods to entertain.

For my spirit lays in ruins,
waiting for the time to once again be refined,
and so I recline as I unwind from my various nightmares.

Time lay claim to my many deposits,

bearing witness to my own emptiness.

Beautiful illusion

The effort it takes to soothe my internal earthquakes,

the breathtaking,
the ever quaking.

Simple times as I chime in mind,

my attempt to unwind.

Hoping is a must,
for my unwavering feelings I just don't trust.

The pressure exist at the expense of my leisure,

though it's the least price to pay,
for setting my spirit and mind astray.

A robust phenomenon,
an untapped and unpredictable mirage,

a warm and sweet disappearance.

A beautiful illusion.

The hat fits

Unapologetic,

such a nice shade.

Wearing it well.

 Grateful when it pays.

 Blisters hidden,

covering the painful days.

Could no longer stand for the days,

sullied by artificial claims.

Grey traits

A lesson to be heard,

before it takes flight.

To the literate of birds,

 that seeks wisdom's teachings.

The bag pack of retention,
along the days we seek to never mention.

The bleeding wounds,

traumatic scenes.

How real is life when darkness blooms.

Tragic

Through the deepest cuts,

such unfiltered sounds,

the crooked rip,

the secret drown.

Life cells to never again tell a tale.
A death of the very memories that once let your soul take flight.

The screams that are never heard.

Oxygen,
and nutrients of your love,

no longer sustain life.

Dark

There is solace in the dark,
all it takes is to turn off the lights that blinds,

the sound that deafens,
oral pause to allow it all to marinate.

Your soul will do the rest

Continuous

The quiet appears,

and seem so poised.

It appears that my mind was screaming,

all this time,
so much noise.

Daunting tides

What a treat when the darkness creeps.

So much zest as it accumulates on numerous amounts of scrap heaps.

Nesting in the outskirts of your subconscious,

waiting for the incentive,
inclined to push towards trust..

At the forefront,
all smiles,
waiting for the boils to subside,

such beautiful gestures,

we would be alright one day;
though we had never defined such period to a specific degree.

No demands in the calm,
and so we stand hand in hand with sweaty palms.

Life process

What's pain to the insane?

Cannon fodder.

 Ammunition and motivation,

all the same.

A mustang, painted in your veins,

 like tattoos giving clues.

Injected fumes.

Extracting your story all the same,

for the world to see.

One day,

maybe it aids or treats.

Wild

Pandemonium.

With a hint of sodium.

Shed tears alleviates nightmares,

that would other wise be potent.

Elevation leaps,

from the shadows.

In the midst of everything,
awaiting the madness to my methods to increase.

Soon it deflates and dissipates in disappointment.

Shrug worn,

every showing,
poised in its form as it keeps waiting.

Ground-hog

The Pain runs deep.

In the belly it creeps.

Like blue veins,

leaving breathlessness,

how insane.

Bottom of the barrel we remain,

centuries passed,
still the same.

Abysmal

It happens right on queue,

 something like the deep blue.

Unscathed thus far by the splinters of your mental blade.

Though like a thousand paper-cuts;
I'm discovering a thousandth bleeding place.

Looking to space,

 bloodshot vision,

 but fading.

Urgency fell upon me,

 I sense I have not long.

Pressure consistent and immense,
senses dense,
squeezing my inners thoughts and emotions from spilling,

like coins of dimes or one and two pence.

Continuance,

 slipping,

here we go again.

Life Trails

Life trails,
following,
the only incentive expectant tales.

Smothered in the aura of adventure,
a mean mug overlooking my times of misfortune,

with a jitter,

a licking lust of excitement,

ever the speech of "so exciting".

Like night at the movies,
life has been drawn in,
the mediocre and uncanny exchange over the decades,

from various unknowns leaves a stain,

characteristics some what deranged.

From when we came

Life in the fast lane,

so prone to pain.

Living in bliss revolving cycles of ultimate reminisce,

 and being free from restraint.

Irrespective is but a spectrum to never be ventured,

thus repercussion needs not be mentioned.

Though to live in a shade of ignorance comes with a price;

once of twice,
your misdeeds like Karma expires overnight.

Dreaming of the days when you see the true flames,

to fear the aspect of heat jumping for a bite once again.

The flesh remain repentant should such a day ever came,

for self expression from within will never be tamed.

Nonetheless,
needless for we are truly in a world of dead skins,

never to be felt in such callous terrain.

Black Rose

Vasoconstriction,

in your vicinity.

Voice hoarse timidly.

Oh,

if but a smile prithee.

Love irrespectively,

pretty thee.

Our passion opens the heavens to revelations,

thus destiny.

Greatness

In the calmness of the warmth,

 your destiny awaits,
it approaches your amazing space.

Special are the times we cannot escape,

for it channels from us,
requirements that one could only hope to approximate.

From break till dawn,

shadow illuminates in excitement.

Even to the point of salivation.

In the process of pontification.

Scorned are pawns that relish your demise,
though the journey in composite with the pain may yet see you through.

One day we shall remain,
laugh in bundles at our unfruitful pulls.

Dark origins

Beauty is amazing if only you can see it.

Special are the times when you can appreciate.

These are the days?
Special is the space,

love remain the place.

Sublime,

inclined to find my mind,

only to find you remain.

Untamed,

unexplained,
in your beauty in its constant.

Like time,

Standing still,
unreal how feelings of your complexities are appealing.

Reeling tapes,
failed attempts to save your amazing grace.

Though,
no place like your amazing space.

Time will tell

From the start to the finish,

where will it ever end.

Time will tell.

Here's to the unclaimed chapters that remain in the remnants of time never
to be ventured again.

In its haunting,
it remains in our psyche like a ghost of an unforgotten past,

never to be realized.

Such are the factors that compels us.

The conveying journeys

In the midst of the journey,
on the way to being what we're suppose to be.

Special are the time that we realise without the onset of the external invite;

anonymous rays,
that filter your plight,
which aids in your wonderment until you see with that necessary level of
clarity.

As it pertains to thee,
there is no us without being firstly;

what we're suppose to be.

Love sense in alteration,
compels to develop the smells that entails the swells to the resulting initial,

and what could only be predicted through destiny.

How lovely.

Painted Pain

No x-rays for saints.

X-amount of paint.

For unforgiven moments,
bones painted in formidable amounts of pain.

In search of remedies.

Wrapped in solitude as the bone creeks.

It covets me,

reminds me of the never ending moments of madness.
The placebo days,
trying to trick oneself.
Hoping to relinquish the by- product of misplaced passionate ways.

Now sitting in a pool redundancy.

Searching for you

In the delusional confines of my mind,
there you will find familiars of the preposterous kind.

Though in the midst,

there you stood...

In all your tangibles.

Screaming it was real.

It took me a while to realise,

 for you stood afar.

Yet as your voice reverberates,

 it was not hard to find.

Belly of the beast

In the hidden depth,

 the belly of the beast.

It looks to me in spite,

begging for some courage to unlock its might.

The process of appeasing does not apply to it,

it wants what hit wants,

everything else is beneath it.

Appetite that spans for generations.

Enough is never enough.

In your Constellation

You're above the stars The ultimate constellation.

I sit afar in omission of your world.

A place of desire,

where I want to be.

Though in your absence,
the world sit in ray of lacklustre.

The clouds that screams out loud,

bursting my ear drums.
My shadow drunk from the melancholic path that you lay at my feet.

Lord knows the world will never be the same.
The world so cold.
Now I stand convinced,

I will never feel again...

In your constellation.

A Sonnet to the stars

A mere chime,
on the conscience of space and time.

Living in subconscious faculties,

hoping;

maybe our smiles could some how render the universe in a feel good
mood,
to extend the day for more play.

Sun in disarray,
for the moon and the neighbour stars,

has never been in the mood to come out and stay.

A sonnet play,
thinking we would never again see you in a state,

more prone to smiles,
as opposed to dismay.

Staying in the moment

Falling back to habits.

Is it not just,
like a portal waiting for the door to open up.

The ever-clutch,
pardon me and my ever changing ways.

It uplifts then plummets,

 almost in a never- ending phase.

Eyes forever lased;
to the target,
the journey ever taken for never- ending days.

Love cometh.

Trying my best to love,

 in the best of ways.

Escapism

An escape artist to the moments that gets to me.

Sometimes I flee and return to the mind scene.

Though for the time being,

no being still,
suffering the ill- will from the venoms,

vampiric essence;

the type that inhibits your steady state.

Tipping away while dripping,

leaving a stain in the process of the sipping.

Life is demeaning,
in the private,

 suffering the bloodshed,

the type that few can imagine.

Chapter 7:WISDOM RAIN

Ink mode

Pen sharp.

Aching for a slice.

Concise with nice.

 Seasoned with emotional grace.

It reiterates its place in the many facets of purpose,

 it represents with grace.

The many places,
journey taken,
lord knows how the universe keeps the corners of my imagination

discovering yet another place.

We tread the bare and with a snare,
we dare to never compare,
for uniqueness is a currency that lacks company.

The soul truth,
the pudding in searching of thee for the ill truth.

The ultimate rebuke.

Mouth sleeps,
but mind never on mute.

Solar Flare

A solar flare.
Highlighting my nightmares,
as it glares and sparks at your brutish remarks.

Left me solemn and mean,
some what untidy and unclean.
A meaning to my leanness,

while I try my best to refrain from the uncalled feelings of not being

blessed.

Life can seem fickle spying through the eye of the pin,

narrow minded and not free,

in a sense shackled with the docile imprints as it attempts even more to get
to me.

Though the onset of choice is my cling to sanity,
the need to be free and live without a melancholic spree,
in the dawn of days,
timid by the maze that stands between your logic and tranquillity.

Inverted

So it appears but is it real?
It may be transparent in a loose sense.

Minute values,
excess amount of calories,
yet scraping below the barrel to find definition.

Spring cleaning to find the existence that defines the epitome of meaning,

therefore extra screening.

Though the traps that lead,

 compels you to sew to find the floor;

discoveries,
there lies the riches for the eyes.

Extra drinking for the extra thirsty.

Brain neighbouring to emotion with momentum leading to motion,

 though no surprise.

Love the senses that make discoveries as it's defined to be.

In the most epic illusions have no form;

for it knows,
sees and does all.

There is no mental retreat for it predicts your mind and all its feats.

Synonymous,

anonymous.

Love,

faith and trust.

Varied time

To the many-pause that comes my way,

 hoping to reap many sewing to flow another day.

Love the kindest of times;
when the wind tells stories of a time that unbeknownst to me.

The tranquil moments that are taken for granted.

We shall bask in the merries,
the queries and not so cheery of times that makes our ponder an adventure.

The mere revelations of times embedded with the ultimate chimes,

that leaves you inclined to gasp for air

Living in the moments that takes your breath away.

Advantage and Terrain

The irony spins in the middle of the room.

Teasing in anticipation,
for the follicles of life is not what it's supposed to be.

Irrevocably,
the things that I was programmed and primed to be.

My conditioning I realised was not what I would like it to be.

Though thankful for the moments,
I am sure it played it's part in the making of me.

Though the time has come to live and let be,

to retreat and repeat repetitively.

Until convoluted are the moments that had their claws in me.

Let them cease and never again let be.
We are the moments of the relics,
the times that leaves no merits,
only typical chimes that leaves you twisted to the point of needing to
unwind.

It swings and sways for days,
moments or pressure on lay-away,
as the suspense built that not only took his breath away.

For the moments were many that saw him seeing plenty,
leaving him mystified and sorry- eyed for his perception of the past is not
what it has been deemed.

Resulting in him being left in a dribbled terrain and excess melancholy.

A pool of toxins of his own making, though never forsaken.

After-all life is what you make it to be.

Thus the periods that had disperses can undoubtedly be reserved;

 making you one with me,
for the eye in I sees far beyond the high and the potential that can
ultimately be.

Instincts

Tapping in,

waiting for a stim(ulation),

 a sudden whim.

A little spillage from the soul somewhere deep within.

There lies a place where the all sparks,

 a conduit like thing.

It permeates for days waiting on the time for releasing.

The sweet swelling...

the compelling.

It knows no bounds,

 unclean for days leaving it smelling.

The funkiest of times,

convoluted rhymes;

stick a pin.

Here goes another day,
lets get back to the world of no dulls or grey.

It reverberates through the colourful,

like the ever mending days.

No spare feelings to keep inspired and flowing.

Slow flows make the heart goes,

how slow or fast nobody knows.

Just the rhymes through our days of ultimate turn and chimes,

the lust and lines of excitement,
it remains uniform over time...

Waiting to show me a new way to think or ultimately get over my timely
ties.

Transcending the meaning of timeless,
for what is the meaning of mind to the mindless.

To the road we press,
awaiting the days our intellectual roads grow finite.

In spite,
we lay in hope to be right,
hoping to never regress to moments that defeats everything we hold dear

to our method of madness.

Nitpicking

The derivative of the unsolved.

Constructed and construed.

Emotions on nude,
screaming the worse of the morbid and crude.

The embodiment of rage leaves an unsavoury plight on the brain.

Cerebral cocktail,
the uncanny and not so plain.

The various stimulus of convoluted memories,

pertaining to indignations and lack of trust.

How robust,

as the linen of your soul slips so low to the very pillage you would never
bear witness,
or hold dear.

Treading lines that left me confined between my mental benign,

negotiations with paranoia.

Growing smart or taller,

there envelopes the need to know,

and so I climb and climb.

Then some.

Back in disarray.

The future seems so far away,
so I thought it best just to settle to survive for another day.

Solitude appears with gazing eyes,
no other takers,
room for manoeuvre or opportune moments,

 thus I assume it's the only way.

Timid to the senses,
on contemplation or contemporary relinquishes,
it seems like a long time but it was only the other day;

So with one synchronized mind,
responding in kind,
I took my place amongst the shadows and shaded gazes...

How sweet they waited for me all this time,
and some what in kind I guess they knew my responses,

 appreciate their efforts and warm welcome.

In between the stars,
mindful as I take a scoop of the dark crevices that never seem to get the
okay.

Like minds responding in kind,

 seeing but never believing,

conceiving but never revealing.

Some minds are better left only for the stars to see,

perhaps then it respond in kind,
bearing the brunt of the darkness that one could get lost in.

Control with finesse

What's it to be,
the cushion or the hammer for thee?

Ultimately,
the games that plagues only goes deeper into the rabbit hole with every
turn.

Every churn,
twisted to the point that makes it hard to breathe;

blood and sweat to my sleeve.

Alleviate to what excess, or do I simply just leave,

to run away and never stay,
or simply running to run another day.

Please don't leave!

The devil you love today maybe more finesse prone,

than the one you meet tomorrow when you run further away.

To whom doth these trees, ants and plants belong.

Don't you see I am but one,
and an island like domain is all I seek.

Suddenly the doors creek,

a sweet patter on the back.

Sensational,
as the heart seeks,

bloody flow creeps,

to the ear drum,

how fun as the ear numb for the self evaluation hath me feeling some what glum.

Wishing I had listen to my shadow and loud flows within my crown,

begging for the days to be numbered,
perhaps one's concept of control will come tumbling down.

Don't forget you

Threading gains to cope with the lame;

through time I rewrite my temporal pain.

Knitting away in the most dazed of days,

nobody but myself,
seconds from ticking away.

Branding my name so I would never forget from whence i came,

the darkness that drained,
along with the gains,
the positive and plain.

A mind-field,
all that I could see was a spine-field in need,

like a graveyard begging to be rescued;

only through a better ending can they proceed,

to dismount,

pause in their distress and uselessly lay claim to lacklustre blame.

The masses of complexes binds to the back like vast acres of trees,

fallen on knees,
waiting for the noise to recede.

Had to sweep,
and sweep,
even through the crevices,

the places that are ever missed.

It compels my senses,
and my complexes,

to carry on,
solely reliant on technique and routine.

Thus,
when the smoke screen inhibits my beam,
I know not of the vision,
yet I remain keen to paddle and not to breathe in my own steam.

Beyond moles there are discoveries, yet they aid me,
facilitating my mishaps and know nots.

Daring for the day I remember me.

Wishful thinking,
that one day maybe life will continue without the feeling of being in need.

Comes and goes with the tide

I pour as it rains.

It envelopes my surroundings,

knowing no bounds.

In a reach to counteract the effects,
but its reliance lacks even the mere concept of vulnerability.

Engraved within its veins you will find immortality.

Blood flows slowly,
falling like grains through a steel arteries;

callous and cold.

To what degree do you reach for the moments that's beyond defeat.

Like the vines in a downward approach,

reaching inward,
constantly reaching for the best of me.

Within the tucked parts that defeats tell tales signs,

 thus nobody could get to me.
Thus lacking air and contact,
praying for the day the cells grow progressively.

Seeing the parts or places relatively,

sighting the parts of their being,

how they had never dreamed it to be;

 how lovely.

When the sentiments run dry,

to what degree to smile.

To what degree to pile quantities of unhappy.
A testament to the wild and inverted thoughts that defies existence,

thus we never think of it.

It passes as it basks between worlds of the depth of the subconscious,

with a sixth sense and a third degree;
when is the right time for thee.

We know not of concrete destiny,
only the cracks of splinters of what not to be.

Drowning in the moments of disappointment of what never was.

Bearing the many faces that do not belong to me,
I can sense them,
they sleep in the crevice between the realms of the subconscious
comfortably.

So prone to the unknown,
the only appeal that for a moment I know not of thee.

The memories come like waves that build with the tide,

set sail in my mind,
open then combust,
shredded to splinters,
disintegrate then never to be seen again.

Perhaps they vacate to a dimension my mind is not privy to,

a cosmic spin.

Last of the Mohican

If not for the exclusivity,
and remote,

the livity,
let love be-spoke.

Speaking truth into the sands of time.

The turning tides that reside inside,

unscrupulous the traits that lay base in your space.

No more are the days when a fix was the test of time.

To lay waste with grace,
honour in the moments we liveth that only the truth can find.

The common is unlike,
thus the world is quite like the flipping kind,

coin toss,
earth trailing to portray our trauma,
the universe implores thee;
life is not forever so be kind.

Unbeknownst the meaning of tomorrow,

 though today there lies no trying,
for we live in the most trying of times,
in our minds,
trying to cope with the utmost you will find.

What's life got to do with it;

everything,
it is the painter and the brush,

the twilight to the highlight,

igniting the everlasting crimes.

Living in the combustibles,
the memories that will heat your mind,
the conscience is belligerent,

perplexed by the abnormal and unsavoury tones,

hard press to predict life's tumbling,
in the midst of your luck's peak.

Revenge is Karma's for the taking.

What is life if not for the concept of time,

the brittle hands,
with a sturdy forearm,
total recall like nobody you will ever find.

Thus a convoluted moment,

we could not help to uncover.

Though we wallow in the blink of an eye with nonchalance,

like our tomorrows are infinite,
so the forgotten will be remembered at later time,

never being too late,
not knowing forgiveness is the game,
and time was never that kind.

As I decompose

Life in a hole,

like a mole,

As a tooth decay,
so ignorant as it sprays.

There you lay,

essential withers,

every single day.

Checking palms,

forever lost in arms,

pondering life.

Lethal injection,

bursting to strive.

The trivial of time,
quite like the never-ending of rhymes.

Telling tales that doth not wish to be silent,

to an audience that does not wish to hear it.

So it happens again,
the hip with strain;
the portrayal of cruel intentions,

thus cracks remains.

Wounded river, bleeding;
over and over again.

It cries water by the tons,
and so its bloody mouth never stains.

Compartmentalised,

societal remnants.

No see no more

Let the lungs of life breathe,

then like an ulcer,
as a tire it punctures.

Leakage of history and the demise of many;

the Ann Franks,

the Benny Ranks.

Did my complexion capture your tongue,
singing the hymns of songs like they have never been sung.

Y et,

another black man.

Pause,
there goes another one.

Cradle to the grave,

the hymn of the unsung.

Fighting for that pivotal day,

that life sings,
giving life to our hymns,

 putting into our narrative,

enough breath to be a song.

Never let them get to me

I won't let them get to me,

 let me lose my cool.

Foot to stool,

turbulent as breeze on a mule.

We are forever,

our essence,

melts away then evaporates,

the ultimate effervescence.

Mucus to the soul,

while I pontificate,
the levels of life,
the X amount of strife.

 Though that's for another day,

positive for I survive.

It brings highlights to my pursuit,
for I persevere,
to heights,
still seeking enlightenment,
and growth,
there is no limit when you refuse to lose.

Now ice in the veins,
so much knowledge that it pains,

 tilt to the head as it strains.

Perhaps it could once again,

 in wonderment,

 blowing cool to the wind.

 Such callous sins.

Natures omniscience,

 though I would never listen,

heed the warnings,
allow the lights to dictate my plight.

No storm nor fright,

unwilling to be polite.

Refusing to stop,
adamant to be heard,
to channel the moments,
the entities that are somewhat dormant.

Plastered walls that tells secret tales,

while we contemplate,
the loud lies that had not needed to be said,

though the debt is paid,

insurmountable folds.

It pitches and stands,

once again attached to my soul.

Let the cold in

Fragmented Chaos.
Explosive culprit like a nuclear holocaust.

Ego's claws viable pairing,

 it was written in the stars.

Scouring the universe,

it scratches and scrapes.

No organic or sincere,

beware.

Nightmares with a lack of sense,

repentance,
with no recompense,

just the absence of sense,

or conscience.

Potential like a bird in a cage.

Bear witness as it takes centre stage.

The moments beckons,
as I become,
numb to the cause and the pain.

Cheeks withdrawn,

melancholic glum.

Clipping thumbs,
waiting for the echoes as they grow,

it was too late,

finite grew restless.

Gripping,
in the millionth and nth,

split second,
trying to tie myself back in.

Although life was made to win,

 time was made to transcend,

and beyond.

Missed yet I sense them lingering,

oscillating,
on the outskirts,

vibrational cheers;
hoping for more wins.

The stars are nought without life's admiration,

thus I sit in awe,
hoping am correct in my stance,
some what trendsetting,
as I seep in the misery in my nucleus;
I can take it.

The journey continues,
undeniable,

 prithee,

 bear no issue.
Hoping to be privy to the more convoluted moments,

perhaps I can aid to let the light in,
and then some.

Where logic meets emotion.

The ultimate potion,
it combines in kind to relinquish the constraints of the mind.

There lies moments of explosion.
In such a premise,
madness is not hard to find.
It binds to the unkind,
like opposites that are naturally inclined.
There lies the ignition,
the potential to be more than.

My plan uplifts,
to the moments that need not be mentioned.

They exist in the mind's unsullied by constraints.

Not afraid to paint to heart's content,
even in the moments that makes no sense.

Logic to paper or paint,
seeing the moments that renders us transparent,

ultimate magnification,

so much so;
even our demons ponders to moments of relent.

For shadows thrive in the darkness away from light.

The black rose,
energy promises to emit and juxtapose,

irrespective of the physical laws.
Through time potential grows and grows.
Like figments,
it ponders in the darkest parts of the ethos.

The murder of reminisce

Those were the days,
in the onset of the many ways;

when life was free,
excuse me...
As my pondering gets lost in tranquillity.

Smile cries,

juxtaposed by my blinding-realise.

The days turns to night,
then back to day overnight.

Firelight,
the super-seams,

in my khaki jeans,
reminds me of the more simpler times,

 so uniform,
so clean.

The epic beam,
from the deepest outskirts,

 through the cracks until it hurt.

Pain so insane for months on end,

till one day suddenly it made sense.

The moon was absent for a reason,

it took to the tides,
so my eyes can realise.

To what do I owe these true lies,

 for no way do I submit to my demise,

under any franchise,
ill-facts to any surprise.

The moments compels for rehab,
bleeding,
nonplussed,
unbeknownst that I had been dabbed.
The wounds carry tell-tales signs,
perhaps underneath my claws,
evidence I will find.
The extra kind that defeats the imagination of any times.

Can't live with the thought of regress,

 it grooms me for the senseless,

 the process of bliss,
unless I desist from reminisce,
no moment is worth all of this.

Better yet,
here comes the part where you no longer exist.

Until I see you again

There is a shift I can feel it.

 Something have changed in the ethos,

lord knows,
so impactful it makes it hard to flow.

So timid I go,
hands on imaginary notes,

 reiterating thoughts from nought.

Tapping in,

profoundness at my finger tips;

stick a pin,

let it settle in.

Waiting for the sorrows,
the uncanny moments making it hard for me to forget.

The moments stay with me,

the emotions constantly,

trying to get me,

waiting for the daunting,
so hard the path to unravel;

hence where do we begin?

Every emotion and experience,

I've felt it all,

so I sit like piece of iron,

the ultimate conduit.

A postural lean,
perhaps my mental cup may over flow at a point and drain.

Though the moments reign,
they stay like a stain,
forever being forced for a mental scrubbing.

My demons see more of me,
more than I see of them,
elements at a trend,
waiting for the day that my spirit could never endure to the point of

content.
Excuse my callousness,

occupied by the thought until I see you again.

R.I.P Jason Carty

THE END

Get a free copy of Into the Abyss Volume 2

Kane began to thrive as he attempted to make a new start with his family. He was happy for the first time in what appeared to be a lifetime of hardship. Little did he know that the web of turmoil was still in play. Will he be able to recover from yet another daunting situation to rescue his loved ones.

Get a free copy of the sequel
Into the Abyss Volume 2
Subscribe to website:
https://dreamimagineexpress.mailchimpsites.com/

About Author

As a creator, poetry was the first form of expression that I was enamoured by, resulting in the captivation of my imagination. It depicts warmth and effervescence painted in colours that only existed in my mind, where I could now translate into poetic art.

The motivating factor for choosing to put my work on display and to share to the masses being the realisation we're all of growth through similar experiences. Nonetheless, we're not always equipped with the tools to articulate, thus making my work very relatable to so many.

To conclude, my writing is my aid, which helps through the worst and best of times.

The goal being to draw from my happiness and pain, in hope you can relate, to further give relief or assist though whatever you're going through.

Dedication To the memory of Jason. Carty

He was a mentor, coach, father, brother, uncle to myself and many more. He bore a significant role in the man I am today, a guide and an accomplice to aid my hand through the very experiences I weathered throughout life that inspired my growth, my processing through my growing pains.

Appreciation

Dedication to the process, the journey, wherever else it may take me for it is an adventure in itself to be a student of the arts. Thus, this was written with the thought that the many audiences that read my story could find tools to help them on their way through their own life experiences.

A moment of thought to the pain, and the moments that drive to periods of realisation, leading to solutions where our trials and situations are concerned.

Printed in Great Britain
by Amazon